Donald Trump

BY DIANE MARCZELY GIMPEL

Published by The Child's World®
1980 Lookout Drive • Mankato, MN 56003-1705
800-599-READ • www.childsworld.com

Photographs ©: Dan Hallman/Invision/AP Images, cover, 1;
Michael Snyder/AP Images, 4; Joseph Sohm/Shutterstock
Images, 7; Beth J. Harpaz/AP Images, 8, 11; Bettmann/Getty
Images, 12; Shutterstock Images, 14; Ric Francis/AP Images,
16; Peter Morgan/Reuters/Newscom, 18; Carlo Allegri/
Reuters/Newscom, 21

ISBN 9781503816497
LCCN 2016954292

Printed in the United States of America
PAO2322

ABOUT THE AUTHOR

Diane Marczely Gimpel is an English
and social studies teacher and a
former newspaper reporter. She holds
a bachelor's degree in journalism
and political science from Duquesne
University and a master's degree in
education from Arcadia University.

Table of Contents

★ ★ ★

TRUMP

DonaldJTrump.com ★ @realDonaldTrump

rida

Donald Trump visited many states during his campaign for president in 2016.

GAIN!

CHAPTER ONE

Trump Runs for President

★ ★ ★

Donald J. Trump is known for many things. He is a **businessman** from New York. He has a bold personality. Trump often speaks his mind.

In 2016, Trump became known for something else. He wanted to change his job. He decided to run for president of the United States.

Americans picked a new president in 2016. At first, 23 people wanted the job. There were six **Democrats**. The other seventeen were **Republicans**.

The Democratic and Republican parties each picked one person. He or she would be the party's choice for president. Some powerful people said Trump would never be chosen. Some voters said they would not pick Trump, either. Trump kept trying anyway.

People in every state voted for one person. Many people voted for Trump. The votes added up. Trump got more than the other Republicans.

In May 2016, everyone was surprised. Trump learned he had enough votes. He would be the Republican **candidate** for president. He was very happy.

The Democrats picked Hillary Clinton. Americans voted on November 8, 2016. Clinton and Trump were the two main choices. It was a close race.

Trump (center) with other Republican candidates in December 2015

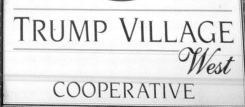

Trump's father, Frederick Trump, earned his fortune by building apartment complexes like this one in Brooklyn, New York.

CHAPTER TWO

Growing Up Trump

★ ★ ★

Donald John Trump was born on June 14, 1946. His family was from New York City. He had two older sisters. He also had an older brother. Another brother was born later. Donald's mother was born in Scotland. Donald's father made money building houses. The Trumps lived in a big house. The house had 23 rooms and nine bathrooms. The family had a maid and a driver.

Donald had rules to follow at home. He was not allowed to eat snacks. He was not allowed to say bad words. He had to eat all of his dinner.

His father taught him about money. Donald sold newspapers to earn money. He worked hard.

Donald liked to have fun, too. He liked to play sports. He liked to go to magic stores with his friend. They bought stink bombs at the shop. They also bought smoke bombs. They even bought hot pepper gum. They played tricks on their friends at school.

Sometimes Donald threw erasers at teachers. He would throw cake at birthday parties. So his parents sent him to a different school. Donald learned how to be serious there. He got good grades. He also played baseball.

After high school, Donald went to college in New York. He learned about business. Then Donald went to a business school in Pennsylvania. He worked for his father during college. He graduated in 1968.

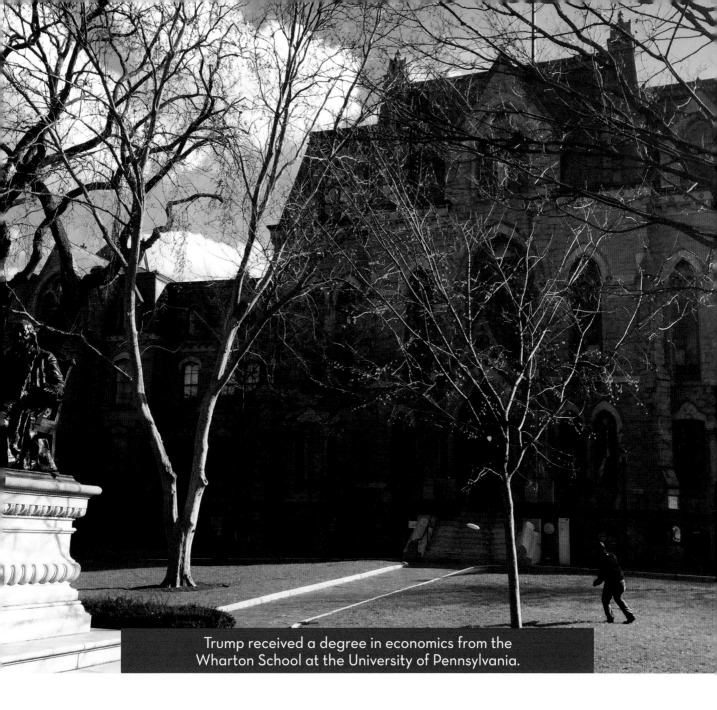

Trump received a degree in economics from the Wharton School at the University of Pennsylvania.

He continued working for his father after school.

Someday he would run his father's business.

Trump holding a model of Trump Tower in 1980

CHAPTER THREE

Trump the Businessman and TV Star

★ ★ ★

At age 25, Trump started running his father's business. He began making deals on buildings. His first big deal was in 1974. He fixed up a hotel. It was in New York City. The updated hotel opened in 1980. People liked it. The hotel made money. Trump became well-known in New York.

In 1983 Trump finished the Trump Tower. It is also in New York. The Trump Tower is a very tall building. It has stores and apartments. It also has a waterfall inside. Trump soon became **famous** across the whole country.

Trump was known for other work, too. He fixed up an ice skating rink. Trump also bought the Plaza Hotel in 1988. He changed it to make it prettier.

Trump built more hotels throughout the 1980s. They were in New Jersey. All of them had his name on them. One was called Trump Plaza. Another was called Trump's Castle. Trump also bought an airline in 1989. He put his name on that, too.

But then Trump was in trouble. He **borrowed** money from banks. He needed the money to build his businesses. But Trump could not pay the banks back. He had to give up some **properties**.

Trump's famous catchphrase on
The Apprentice was, "You're fired."

One bank got a hotel. Another bank got his big, fancy boat. Later his businesses got better.

Then Trump starred in his own television shows. One was called *The Apprentice*. The other was *The Celebrity Apprentice*. The shows were a game. People tried to win a job with Trump. Millions of people watched.

Trump owns buildings all over the world. He also owns golf courses. He is very rich. Many people know Trump because of his businesses. Some of those people thought he should be president.

Trump went on a television show in October 1999
to announce his plans to run for president.

CHAPTER FOUR

Trump Becomes President

★ ★ ★

Trump first thought about running for president in 1988. He wanted to run in 2000, too. He planned to run for the **Reform Party**. Trump later decided not to. He thought there were problems within the party.

Trump thought about running for president many times. Many people wanted Trump to run in 2012. But he said no.

In June 2015, Trump finally decided to run. Trump said the United States was in trouble.

He said the country needed help making deals. Trump wanted to "Make America great again."

Trump made many promises. He wanted to change U.S. health care. He wanted to tax certain American companies. These companies make goods cheaply in other countries. Then they sell them in the United States.

Trump also said he wanted to build a wall. It would be on the southern U.S. border. He wanted to stop people from entering the country. He said these people were coming **illegally**.

Some people did not like what Trump said. They stopped working with him. Others thought Trump did not tell the truth. They also thought he said mean things. Yet many other people liked him. They said he would help the United States. Some believed he would fix the country's money problems.

Some people liked that Trump did not have a background in politics.

Many liked that he said his thoughts out loud. Even if it made others angry. They thought Trump was truthful. They said other candidates were not.

These people helped Trump beat Hillary Clinton. In January 2017, Trump became the 45th president of the United States.

1940

← **June 14, 1946** Donald John Trump is born.

← **1968** Trump graduates from the University of Pennsylvania.

← **1974** Trump makes his first major business deal.

← **February 14, 1983** Trump Tower is completed.

← **1991** Trump files for bankruptcy for the first time.

← **2000** Trump first considers running for president for the Reform Party, but drops out of the election.

← **January 3, 2008** *The Apprentice* airs on TV for the first time.

← **June 2015** Trump decides to run for president.

← **May 26, 2016** Trump learns he has enough votes to become the Republican presidential nominee.

← **July 19, 2016** Trump is announced as the official Republican candidate for president.

← **November 8, 2016** Trump is elected to be the 45th president of the United States.

← **January 20, 2017** Trump is sworn in as president.

2017

borrowed (BOR-ohd) When something is borrowed, it is used temporarily and then given back. Trump borrowed money from the banks for his buildings.

businessman (BIZ-niss-man) A businessman is a person who works to make money. Trump is a businessman who buys land and builds buildings.

candidate (KAN-duh-date) A candidate is a person who is trying to be elected to office. Some people thought Trump was an honest candidate.

Democrats (DEM-uh-kratz) Democrats are people who belong to the Democratic political party. Democrats chose Hillary Clinton to run for president.

famous (FAY-muhss) When someone is famous, they are well-known by many people. Trump became famous for his work on New York City buildings.

illegally (i-LEE-gul-lee) When something is done illegally, it is breaking the law. Trump wanted to build a wall to stop people from crossing the border into the United States illegally.

properties (PROP-ur-teez) Properties are things that a person owns. When Trump owed money to the banks, he had to give up some of his properties.

Reform Party (ree-FORM PAR-tee) The Reform Party is a moderate and populist political party in the United States. Trump thought about running for president for the Reform Party.

Republicans (ri-PUHB-li-kuhnz) Republicans are people who belong to the Republican political party. Republicans chose Trump to run for president.

In the Library

Brown, Fannie T. *Who Is President?* Bloomington, IN:
Trafford Publishing, 2011.

Calkhoven, Laurie. *I Grew Up to Be President.*
New York: Scholastic Inc., 2011.

Piven, Hanoch. *What Presidents Are Made Of.* New York:
Antheneum Books for Young Readers, 2012.

On the Web

Visit our Web site for links about
Donald Trump: **childsworld.com/links**

*Note to Parents, Teachers, and Librarians: We routinely verify our Web links to make
sure they are safe and active sites. So encourage your readers to check them out!*

INDEX